The
Wiersbe
BIBLE STUDY SERIES

JOB

The
Wiersbe
BIBLE STUDY SERIES

Waiting

on God

in Difficult

Times

transforming lives together

THE WIERSBE BIBLE STUDY SERIES: JOB
Published by David C Cook
4050 Lee Vance View
Colorado Springs, CO 80918 U.S.A.

David C Cook Distribution Canada
55 Woodslee Avenue, Paris, Ontario, Canada N3L 3E5

David C Cook U.K., Kingsway Communications
Eastbourne, East Sussex BN23 6NT, England

David C Cook and the graphic circle C logo
are registered trademarks of Cook Communications Ministries.

All excerpts taken from *Be Patient,* second edition, published by David C
Cook in 2009 © 1991 Warren W. Wiersbe, ISBN 978-1-4347-6741-7.

ISBN 978-0-7814-0634-5
eISBN 978-0-7814-0786-1

© 2011 Warren W. Wiersbe

The Team: Steve Parolini, Karen Lee-Thorp, Amy Konyndyk,
Nick Lee, Jack Campbell, Karen Athen
Series Cover Design: John Hamilton Design
Cover Photo: Veer (AYP0608959)

Printed in the United States of America
First Edition 2011

1 2 3 4 5 6 7 8 9 10

072911

Contents

Introduction to Job

Lessons from Suffering

"You have heard of Job's perseverance [endurance]" (James 5:11). Yes, many people have heard about Job and his trials; but not many people understand what those trials were all about and what God was trying to accomplish. Nor do they realize that Job suffered as he did so that God's people today might learn from his experiences how to be patient in suffering and endure to the end.

The book of Job magnifies the sovereignty of God. From the very first chapter, it is obvious that God is in control, for even Satan is told what he can and cannot do. During the debate among Job and his friends, it appears that God is absent, but He is aware of how Job feels and what Job and his friends say. Thirty-one times in the book of Job God is called "the Almighty." Elihu was right on target: God is sovereign and cannot do wrong.

Through the Furnace

Like Job, you may have to go through the furnace in order to study the book and really grasp its message. If so, don't be afraid! By faith, just say with Job, "But he knows the way that I take; when he has tested me, I will come forth as gold" (Job 23:10). Gold fears no fire.

As we study the book of Job together, I trust that two things will be accomplished in your life: You will learn to be patient in your trials, and you will learn how to help others in their trials. Your world is filled with people who need encouragement, and God may be preparing you for just that ministry.

—*Warren W. Wiersbe*

How to Use This Study

This study is designed for both individual and small-group use. We've divided it into eight lessons—each references one or more chapters in Warren W. Wiersbe's commentary *Be Patient* (second edition, David C Cook, 2009). While reading *Be Patient* is not a prerequisite for going through this study, the additional insights and background Wiersbe offers can greatly enhance your study experience.

The **Getting Started** questions at the beginning of each lesson offer you an opportunity to record your first thoughts and reactions to the study text. This is an important step in the study process as those "first impressions" often include clues about what it is your heart is longing to discover.

The bulk of the study is found in the **Going Deeper** questions. These dive into the Bible text and, along with helpful excerpts from Wiersbe's commentary, help you examine not only the original context and meaning of the verses but also modern application.

Looking Inward narrows the focus down to your personal story. These intimate questions can be a bit uncomfortable at times, but don't shy away from honesty here. This is where you are asked to stand before the mirror of God's Word and look closely at what you see. It's the place to take a good look at yourself in light of the lesson and search for ways in which you can grow in faith.

Going Forward is the place where you can commit to paper those things you want or need to do in order to better live out the discoveries you made in the Looking Inward section. Don't skip or skim through this. Take the time to really consider what practical steps you might take to move closer to Christ. Then share your thoughts with a trusted friend who can act as an encourager and accountability partner.

Finally, there is a brief **Seeking Help** section to close the lesson. This is a reminder for you to invite God into your spiritual-growth process. If you choose to write out a prayer in this section, come back to it as you work through the lesson and continue to seek the Holy Spirit's guidance as you discover God's will for your life.

Tips for Small Groups

A small group is a dynamic thing. One week it might seem like a group of close-knit friends. The next it might seem more like a group of uncomfortable strangers. A small-group leader's role is to read these subtle changes and adjust the tone of the discussion accordingly.

Small groups need to be safe places for people to talk openly. It is through shared wrestling with difficult life issues that some of the greatest personal growth is discovered. But in order for the group to feel safe, participants need to know it's okay *not* to share sometimes. Always invite honest disclosure, but never force someone to speak if he or she isn't comfortable doing so. (A savvy leader will follow up later with a group member who isn't comfortable sharing in a group setting to see if a one-on-one discussion is more appropriate.)

Have volunteers take turns reading excerpts from Scripture or from the commentary. The more each person is involved even in the mundane tasks, the more they'll feel comfortable opening up in more meaningful ways.

The leader should watch the clock and keep the discussion moving. Sometimes there may be more Going Deeper questions than your group can cover in your available time. If you've had a fruitful discussion, it's okay to move on without finishing everything. And if you think the group is getting bogged down on a question or has taken off on a tangent, you can simply say, "Let's go on to question 5." Be sure to save at least ten to fifteen minutes for the Going Forward questions.

Finally, soak your group meetings in prayer—before you begin, during as needed, and always at the end of your time together.

The Drama
(JOB 1—3)

Before you begin …
- *Pray for the Holy Spirit to reveal truth and wisdom as you go through this lesson.*
- *Read Job 1—3. This lesson references chapter 1 in* Be Patient. *It will be helpful for you to have your Bible and a copy of the commentary available as you work through this lesson.*

Getting Started

From the Commentary

Job was "perfect and upright" (Job 1:1). He was not sinless, for nobody can claim that distinction, but he was complete and mature in character and "straight" in conduct. The word translated "perfect" is related to "integrity," another important word in Job (2:3, 9; 27:5; 31:6). People with integrity are whole persons, without hypocrisy or duplicity. In the face of his friends' accusations and God's

silence, Job maintained his integrity, and the Lord ultimately vindicated him.

—*Be Patient*, page 17

1. What evidence do we have that Job was "perfect and upright"? Why is this critical to his story? What is the difference between someone who is upright and someone who is sinless?

More to Consider: The events in Job took place during the Patriarchal Age, when a large family was seen as a blessing from God (Gen. 12:2; 13:16; 30:1). How is this significant to the message in Job? How might the story play out differently in today's Western culture?

2. Choose one verse or phrase from Job 1—3 that stands out to you. This could be something you're intrigued by, something that makes you uncomfortable, something that puzzles you, something that resonates with you, or just something you want to examine further. Write that here.

Going Deeper

From the Commentary

While it is true that his three friends hurt Job deeply and wronged him greatly, they were still his friends. When they heard about Job's calamities, they traveled a long distance to visit him, and they sat in silence as they sympathized with him. Their mistake was in thinking they had to explain Job's situation and tell him how to change it.

"My best friend," said Henry Ford, "is the one who brings out the best in me," but Job's friends brought out the worst in him. However, in the end Job and his friends were reconciled (42:7–10), and I like to think that their relationship was deeper than before. To have true friends is to be wealthy indeed.

—*Be Patient*, pages 18–19

3. Read Job 2:11–13. What can we learn about Job's friends by the way they responded when they heard he was troubled? What can we discern about their relationship to Job by their initial reaction to him when they arrived?

From the Commentary

> In one day, Job was stripped of his wealth. One after
> another, four frightened messengers reported that 500
> yoke of oxen, 500 donkeys, and 3,000 camels were stolen
> in enemy raids; 7,000 sheep were struck by lightning
> and killed; and all 10 of his children were killed by a.
> windstorm. King Solomon was right: "Moreover, no man
> knows when his hour will come: As fish are caught in a
> cruel net, or birds are taken in a snare, so men are trapped
> by evil times that fall unexpectedly upon them" (Eccl.
> 9:12 NIV).
>
> Job knew *what* had happened, but he did not know *why* it
> had happened; and that is the crux of the matter. Because
> the author allows us to visit the throne room of heaven
> and hear God and Satan speak, we know who caused
> the destruction and why he was allowed to cause it. But
> if we did not have this insight, we would probably take
> the same approach as Job's friends and blame Job for the
> tragedy.
>
> —*Be Patient*, page 19

4. Review Job 1:6–19. What are some of the truths that emerge from this
scene? What can we learn about God here? What can we learn about Satan
(particularly his access to God)? Why are these truths important to Job's
story? To ours today?

From Today's World

There are plenty of stories throughout history of wealthy men and women who have been suddenly stripped of all their worldly goods. This happened to many people during the stock market slide that precipitated the Great Depression. It happens to stars and celebrities and other people in the public eye constantly. And it happens time and again in a world where natural disasters can wipe out nearly everything in the blink of an eye.

5. How is the loss of everything different in Job's case than in the many stories of others who've lost everything? Did God play a role in the other stories? Did Satan? What leads you to your conclusions?

From the Commentary

God's statement in Job 1:8 echoes the description of Job in verse 1, but Satan questioned it. The word *Satan* means "adversary, one who opposes the law." This is a courtroom scene, and God and Satan each deliver different verdicts about Job. As you study this book, keep in mind that God said "Not guilty!" (1:8; 2:3; 42:7). There was nothing in Job's life that compelled God to cause him to suffer. But Satan said "Guilty!" because he is the accuser of God's people and finds nothing good in them (Zech. 3; Rev. 12:10).

—*Be Patient*, page 20

6. In what ways was Satan's attack on Job really an attack against God? What was Satan's argument? How did Job's friends actually support Satan's argument?

From the Commentary

The hosts of heaven and of hell watched to see how Job would respond to the loss of his wealth and his children. He expressed his grief in a manner normal for that day, for God expects us to be human (1 Thess. 4:13). After all, even Jesus wept (John 11:35). But then Job worshipped God and uttered a profound statement of faith (Job 1:21).

First, he *looked back* to his birth: "Naked came I out of my mother's womb." Everything Job owned was given to him by God, and the same God who gave it had the right to take it away. Job simply acknowledged that he was a steward.

Then Job *looked ahead* to his death: "and naked shall I return." He would not return to his mother's womb, because that would be impossible. He would go to "Mother Earth," be buried, and turn to dust. (The connection between "birth" and "Mother Earth" is seen also in Ps. 139:13–15.) Nothing that he acquired between his birth and death would go with him into the next world. Paul wrote, "For we brought nothing into this world, and it is certain we can carry nothing out" (1 Tim. 6:7).

Finally, Job *looked up* and uttered a magnificent statement of faith: "The LORD gave, and the LORD hath taken away; blessed be the name of the LORD" (Job 1:21). Instead of cursing God, as Satan said Job would do, Job blessed the Lord!

—*Be Patient*, pages 21–22

7. Review Job 1:20–22. Was Job's response to his loss unusual? Why or why not? What response did Satan expect? Job's friends? What was the basis for Job's response?

From the Commentary

> Satan does not give up easily, for he returned to God's throne to accuse Job again. As in the first meeting (1:8), it is God who brings up the subject of His servant Job; and Satan accepts the challenge. We get the impression that God is confident His servant will not fail the test.
>
> "Every man has his price," said Satan. "Job can raise another family and start another business because he still has health and strength. Let me touch his body and take away his health, and You will soon hear him curse You to Your face."

—*Be Patient*, page 22

8. Review Job 2:1–8. How does this passage illustrate Satan's persistence? What does this teach us about Job's trust in God? About how we ought to prepare our hearts for Satan's attacks? Is it true that "every man has his price"? Why or why not?

More to Consider: Read 1 Corinthians 10:13. How does this verse shed light on the relationship between God and Satan? Why is this significant in Job's story? In our stories today?

From the Commentary

If ever a believer in Old Testament days shared in the fellowship of Christ's sufferings, it was Job. All that he humanly had left was his wife and his three friends, and even they turned against him. No wonder Job felt that God had deserted him!

"Curse God and die!" was exactly what Satan wanted Job to do, and Job's wife put the temptation before her husband. Yes, Satan can work through people who are dear to us (Matt. 16:22–23; Acts 21:10–14); and the temptation is stronger because we love them so much. Adam listened to Eve (Gen. 3:6, 12), and Abraham listened to Sarah (Gen. 16); but Job did not listen to the advice of his wife.

—*Be Patient*, page 23

9. Why did Job's wife encourage him to turn against God? Why didn't he listen to her? What does this teach us about the way we're sometimes tested? What does it teach us about what it really means to trust God?

From the Commentary

> Job shares a secret at the close of his lament (3:25–26):
> Before all his troubles started, he had a feeling—and a
> fear—that something terrible was going to happen. Was
> it an intuition from the Lord? Sometimes God's people
> have these intuitions, and it motivates them to seek God's
> face and pray for His help. Is that what Job did? We don't
> know, but we do know that he was a broken man whose
> worst fears had now been realized.
>
> —*Be Patient*, page 27

10. Is it significant that Job sensed something might happen to him? Why
or why not? How might God have helped to prepare Job for this? What
does this tell us about listening to our own intuition?

Looking Inward

Take a moment to reflect on all that you've explored thus far in this study
of Job 1—3. Review your notes and answers and think about how each of
these things matters in your life today.

Tips for Small Groups: To get the most out of this section, form pairs or trios and have group members take turns answering these questions. Be honest and as open as you can in this discussion, but most of all, be encouraging and supportive of others. Be sensitive to those who are going through particularly difficult times and don't press for people to speak if they're uncomfortable doing so.

11. Do you consider yourself "perfect and upright" like Job? If not, why not? What are some reasons Satan might choose you as a target for a similar attack? What are some reasons he might not choose you? How prepared would you be for that attack?

12. What are some of the worst losses you've endured? How did your faith help you through these times? How was your faith challenged?

13. Do you get intuitions about "bad things" that might happen? If so, what do you do with these intuitions? How can they turn you toward God?

Going Forward

14. Think of one or two things that you have learned that you'd like to work on in the coming week. Remember that this is all about quality, not quantity. It's better to work on one specific area of life and do it well than to work on many and do poorly (or to be so overwhelmed that you simply don't try).

Do you want to learn how to prepare for Satan's attacks? Be specific. Go back through Job 1—3 and put a star next to the phrase or verse that is most encouraging to you. Consider memorizing this verse.

Real-Life Application Ideas: The story of Job is more than a story about enduring suffering, but the theme of suffering is certainly at the forefront. Consider people you know who are enduring trials. What are some practical ways you can be a supportive friend to those people? Come up with actionable ideas that can offer comfort and wisdom, then reach out to those people. Try not to be like Job's friends!

Seeking Help

15. Write a prayer below (or simply pray one in silence), inviting God to work on your mind and heart in those areas you've noted above. Be honest about your desires and fears.

Notes for Small Groups:
- *Look for ways to put into practice the things you wrote in the Going Forward section. Talk with other group members about your ideas and commit to being accountable to one another.*
- *During the coming week, ask the Holy Spirit to continue to reveal truth to you from what you've read and studied.*
- *Before you start the next lesson, read Job 4—10. For more in-depth lesson preparation, read chapters 2 and 3, "Discussion Begins" and "The Discussion Continues," in* Be Patient.

The Discussion
(JOB 4—10)

Before you begin ...
- *Pray for the Holy Spirit to reveal truth and wisdom as you go through this lesson.*
- *Read Job 4—10. This lesson references chapters 2 and 3 in* Be Patient. *It will be helpful for you to have your Bible and a copy of the commentary available as you work through this lesson.*

Getting Started

From the Commentary

The three friends were silent for seven days (Job 2:13), and Job later wished they had stayed that way (13:5). "Then Eliphaz, the Temanite, answered [Job]." But what did he answer? The pain in Job's heart? No, he answered the words from Job's lips; *and this was a mistake.* A wise counselor and comforter must listen with the heart and respond to feelings as well as to words. You do not heal a broken heart with logic; you heal a broken heart with

love. Yes, you must speak the truth; but be sure to speak
the truth in love (Eph. 4:15).

—*Be Patient*, page 35

1. Why do you think Job's friends were silent for seven days? Why did they
take a logical approach to their friend's troubles? What does this imply
about their relationship with Job?

*More to Consider: Eliphaz put great faith in tradition (Job 15:18–19),
and the God he worshipped was an inflexible lawgiver. How is this
approach similar to the way the Pharisees related to Jesus? What does
this approach misunderstand about God?*

2. Choose one verse or phrase from Job 4—10 that stands out to you.
This could be something you're intrigued by, something that makes you
uncomfortable, something that puzzles you, something that resonates with
you, or just something you want to examine further. Write that here.

Going Deeper

From the Commentary

> Eliphaz's approach seems to start out positive enough, even gentle; but it was only honey to prepare Job for the bitterness that would follow. "If someone ventures a word with you, will you be impatient?" he asked (Job 4:2 NIV).
>
> "Don't get upset, Job!" is what he was saying. "In the past, your words have been a help to many people; and we want our words to be a help to you."
>
> Never underestimate the power of words to encourage people in the battles of life. James Moffatt translates Job 4:4, "Your words have kept men on their feet." The right words, spoken at the right time, and with the right motive, can make a tremendous difference in the lives of others. Your words can nourish those who are weak and encourage those who are defeated. But your words can also hurt those who are broken and only add to their burdens, so be careful what you say and how you say it.
>
> —*Be Patient*, pages 35–36

3. Review Eliphaz's rebuke in Job 4—5. Why was he so quick to become bitter toward Job? How might Eliphaz have presented the same argument in a gentler manner? Is it possible to offer rebuke in a kind way? Explain.

From the Commentary

Eliphaz's second argument is based on his own personal observations of life (5:1–7). He has seen sinners prosper and take root, only to be destroyed and lose everything. This was a not-so-subtle description of Job's situation. It must have hurt Job deeply to hear that it was his sin that killed his children. But in Psalm 73, Asaph takes a wholly different view. He concludes that God allows the wicked to prosper in this life because it's the only "heaven" they will know. God will adjust things in the next life and see to it that His people are rewarded and the wicked are punished.

—*Be Patient*, page 37

4. What's the danger of making an argument solely from observation? How is God often left out of that argument? How does the fact that God offers judgment according to His timetable and not ours impact our own ability to determine God's ways?

From the Commentary

> Eliphaz closes his speech with words of assurance. The same God who wounds will also heal (Deut. 32:39; Hos. 6:1–2). He will deliver you from trouble, save you from your enemies, and give you a long and happy life and a peaceful death. "We have examined this, and it is true. So hear it and apply it to yourself" (Job 5:27 NIV).

> —*Be Patient*, page 38

5. Review Job 5:17–27. In what ways is Eliphaz's summary more akin to Satan's philosophy than God's? What's wrong with making a bargain with God? How would that have vindicated Satan?

From the Commentary

> Only Eliphaz had spoken so far, but Job could tell that Bildad and Zophar agreed with him. Not one of his friends identified with what Job was going through physically and emotionally. It was one thing for them to sit where he sat and quite something else for them to feel

what he felt (Ezek. 3:15). The child who defined "sympa-thy" as "your pain in my heart" knew more about giving comfort than did these three.

To begin with, they didn't feel the *heaviness* of his suffering (Job 6:1–3). No wonder Job had spoken so impetuously! His friends would have done the same thing if they carried the load that he carried. Job didn't have the full revelation of heaven that believers have today, so his future was dim. We can read 2 Corinthians 4:16–18 and take heart.

—*Be Patient*, pages 38–39

6. In what ways did Job feel like a target? Why didn't Job's friends understand the bitterness of his suffering? (See Job 6:4–7.) What does chapter 6 reveal about the role of sympathy in God's economy?

From the Commentary

Job used several vivid pictures to describe the *futility* of life. He felt like a man who had been conscripted into the army against his will (Job 7:1a, "appointed time"), and like a laborer (v. 1b) or a hired man waiting for sunset and his daily wages (v. 2). At least these men had something to look forward to, but Job's future was hopeless. His nights were sleepless, his days were futile (Deut. 28:67), and the Lord didn't seem to care.

He then focused on the *brevity* of life. Time was passing swiftly; so, if God were going to do anything, He had better hurry! Job's life was like the weaver's shuttle (Job 7:6), moving swiftly with the thread running out. (The phrase *cut me off* in 6:9 means "to cut a weaving from the loom." See Isa. 38:12.) Life is like a weaving, and only God can see the total pattern and when the work is finished.

Job also saw his life as a breath or a cloud, here for a brief time and then gone forever, never to return (Job 7:7–10; James 4:14). God was treating him like a dangerous monster that had to be watched every minute (Job 7:11–12). No wonder Job was bitter against God for guarding him constantly. The fact that Job referred to *Yam* ("the sea") and *Tammin* ("a whale"), two mythological characters, didn't mean he was giving his approval to the teachings of Eastern myths. He used these well-known characters only to illustrate his point.

There was no way Job could escape God, the "watcher of men" (7:20 NIV, NKJV). If Job went to sleep, God frightened him in his dreams. If he was awake, he knew God's eye was upon him (10:14; 13:27; 31:4). He couldn't even swallow his spittle without God knowing about it! Why would God pay so much attention to one man (7:17–18; Ps. 8:4)?

—*Be Patient*, pages 40–41

7. What was Job's main plea in chapter 7? Why did he feel like life was futile? What is the significance of his closing the appeal with a request for forgiveness (7:20–21)?

From the Commentary

"Your words are a blustering wind!" (Job 8:2 NIV). Can you imagine a counselor saying that to a suffering individual who wanted to die? Bildad did; in fact, he used the same approach in his next speech (18:2). Job had poured out his grief and was waiting to hear a sympathetic word, but his friend said that Job's speech was just so much hot air.

—*Be Patient*, page 45

8. What arguments did Bildad present? (See Job 8:1–7; 8:8–10; and 8:11–22.) In what ways did he ignore Job's needs in these arguments? How were Bildad's arguments like sermons instead of responses to a hurting friend?

More to Consider: Bildad didn't quote from the ancients; he knew that Job was as familiar with the past as he was. But Bildad made it clear that he respected the wisdom of the ancients more than the teachings of his contemporaries. How is this argument still being made in churches today? Is there validity to it? Why or why not?

From the Commentary

In Job 9 and 10, Job asks three questions: "How can I be righteous before God?" (9:1–13), "How can I meet God in court?" (vv. 14–35), and "Why was I born?" (10:1–22; see v. 18). You can see how these questions connect. Job is righteous, but he has to prove it…. But if God doesn't step in and testify on Job's behalf, what is the purpose of all this suffering? Why was Job even born?

—*Be Patient*, page 49

9. Is it possible for a mortal man to prove himself righteous before God? Explain. Why did Job ask such difficult questions? What was the purpose of his pondering?

From the Commentary

> Job's argument in 10:1–22 is that God made him and gave him life (vv. 3, 8–12, 18–19), but God was not treating him like one of His own creations. After putting time and effort into making Job, God was destroying him! Furthermore, God was judging Job without even telling him what the charges were against him (v. 2).
>
> —*Be Patient*, page 51

10. Why did Job speak directly to God (instead of to his friends) in his argument about why he was even born (10:1–22)? How was Job feeling when he asked the question, "Why was I even born"? (See 10:1, 15.) How would you answer Job's question?

Looking Inward

Take a moment to reflect on all that you've explored thus far in this study of Job 4—10. Review your notes and answers and think about how each of these things matters in your life today.

> *Tips for Small Groups: To get the most out of this section, form pairs or trios and have group members take turns answering these questions. Be honest and as open as you can in this discussion, but most of all, be encouraging and supportive of others. Be sensitive to those who are going through particularly difficult times and don't press for people to speak if they're uncomfortable doing so.*

11. Have you ever been rebuked by a well-meaning friend? What was that experience like? Did your friend's argument have merit? How did you react to the rebuke? How would you like to respond to future rebukes?

12. Have you ever felt like life was futile? What prompted that feeling? How did your relationship with God affect this season of life? How did your faith help you through it?

13. Have you ever preached to a friend in need instead of offering loving care and concern? What is the right approach to take when a friend is suffering? What if the friend is suffering because of apparent wrong choices?

Going Forward

14. Think of one or two things that you have learned that you'd like to work on in the coming week. Remember that this is all about quality, not quantity. It's better to work on one specific area of life and do it well than to work on many and do poorly (or to be so overwhelmed that you simply don't try).

Do you want to be a better friend to someone who is suffering? Be specific. Go back through Job 4—10 and put a star next to the phrase or verse that is most encouraging to you. Consider memorizing this verse.

Real-Life Application Ideas: Think about your closest friends. Take a moment to consider what sort of friend you're being to them. Are you loving? Patient? Judgmental? Do you tend to preach when they're going through tough times? Talk with your friends and learn how you can be a better friend in times of need. Perhaps what they need most is simply your time, your prayers, and your love.

Seeking Help

15. Write a prayer below (or simply pray one in silence), inviting God to work on your mind and heart in those areas you've noted above. Be honest about your desires and fears.

Notes for Small Groups:

- *Look for ways to put into practice the things you wrote in the Going Forward section. Talk with other group members about your ideas and commit to being accountable to one another.*

- *During the coming week, ask the Holy Spirit to continue to reveal truth to you from what you've read and studied.*

- *Before you start the next lesson, read Job 11—17. For more in-depth lesson preparation, read chapters 4 and 5, "An Angry 'Younger' Man" and "Discussion Turns into Dispute," in* Be Patient.

The Dispute
(JOB 11—17)

Before you begin …
- *Pray for the Holy Spirit to reveal truth and wisdom as you go through this lesson.*
- *Read Job 11—17. This lesson references chapters 4 and 5 in* Be Patient. *It will be helpful for you to have your Bible and a copy of the commentary available as you work through this lesson.*

Getting Started

From the Commentary

Job's three friends were old men, so Zophar must have been the youngest since he spoke last. His first speech is not long; but what it lacks in length, it makes up for in animosity, for it reveals that Zophar was angry. There is a proper time and place for the display of righteous anger (Eph. 4:26), but Job's ash heap was not the place, and that was not the right time. "The wrath of man does not produce the righteousness of God" (James 1:20 NKJV). What Job needed was a helping hand, not a slap in the face.

—*Be Patient*, page 59

1. What are the three accusations Zophar made against Job (11:1–4; 11:5–12; 11:13–20)? How did Job answer these accusations (Job 12)?

More to Consider: Read Romans 12:15. How might Zophar's speech to Job have been different if he'd thought to "mourn with those who mourn"?

2. Choose one verse or phrase from Job 11—17 that stands out to you. This could be something you're intrigued by, something that makes you uncomfortable, something that puzzles you, something that resonates with you, or just something you want to examine further. Write that here.

Going Deeper

From the Commentary

> Job is ignorant of God (Job 11:5–12). Zophar's request in verse 5 was answered when God appeared (38:1); but it was Zophar and his two friends who were later rebuked by God, and not Job! Job was commended by the Lord for telling the truth. Beware of asking God to tell others what they need to know, unless you are willing for Him to show you what *you* need to know.
>
> Zophar wanted Job to grasp the height, depth, breadth, and length of God's divine wisdom (11:8–9). In saying this, Zophar was hinting that he himself already knew the vast dimensions of God's wisdom and could teach Job if he would listen.
>
> —*Be Patient*, page 60

3. What did Zophar mean when he said the secrets of God's wisdom were two sided (Job 11:6)? Read Ephesians 3:17–19. How does what Zophar said in Job 11:7–8 contradict the truth of this passage?

From the Commentary

"There is hope!" is Zophar's encouraging word to Job (11:18), and he described what Job could experience. God would bless him abundantly, and his troubles would be over. Job could lift up his head again, and his fears would be gone (v. 15; 10:15). He would forget his misery like water gone over the dam (11:16). God would give him a long life, and it would be the dawning of a new day for him (v. 17). He would dwell in the light, not in the darkness of Sheol (10:20–22); and God's security would put an end to all his fears (11:19–20).

But if Job wanted these blessings, he had to get them on Zophar's terms. Yes, there was hope, but it was hope with a condition attached to it: Job must repent and confess his sins (vv. 13–14). *Zophar is tempting Job to bargain with God so he can get out of his troubles.* This is exactly what Satan wanted Job to do! "Doth Job fear God for nought?" Satan asked (1:9). Satan accused Job of having a "commercial faith" that promised prosperity in return for obedience.

—*Be Patient*, pages 61–62

4. Review Job 11:13–20. What would Job's story have been if he'd followed Zophar's advice? What does 13:15 tell us about the kind of faith Job had?

From Today's World

Public figures have always been targets for naysayers, those who disagree with their beliefs or policies. But in today's society, the speed at which news (and lies) can travel has increased to the point where it's nearly instantaneous. An accusation against a public figure can, within minutes, be viewed by millions, thanks to social media and 24-7 cable news networks. Truth and lies alike fly across the Internet faster than any small-town rumor mill ever could ever hope for.

5. How has the Internet age changed the way people disagree with one another? How has it affected the way people express their opinions on spiritual matters? What are the benefits of this new age of information? What are the dangers? How might Job's story have been different had it occurred in this modern age? What role would the Internet play?

From the Commentary

> Zophar's speech was a brief one, but Job took a long time to answer each of Zophar's accusations. Job began with Zophar's second accusation that Job had no knowledge of God (Job 11:5–12). Job affirmed that he had wisdom and understanding just as they did (Job 12). Then he replied

to Zophar's first accusation that Job was a guilty sinner
(11:1–4). Job once again affirmed his integrity (Job 13).
Job then closed his speech by challenging Zophar's third
point, that there was still hope (11:13–20). In Job 14, Job
admits that his hope is almost gone.

—*Be Patient*, page 62

6. Why did Job take so much time to respond to Zophar's speech? What is
the general tone of his response? What does this tell us about Job's attitude
toward Zophar? Toward God?

From the Commentary

In his first speech (Job 4—5), Eliphaz had displayed some
kindness toward Job, but you find neither patience nor
kindness in this second address. Nor do you find any new
ideas: Eliphaz merely repeats his former thesis that man
is a sinner and God must punish sinners (5:17–19). He
issued two warnings to Job.

(1) Job lacks wisdom (Job 15:1–16).

(2) God judges the wicked (Job 15:17–35).

—*Be Patient*, pages 72, 74

7. Review Job 15. On what basis did Eliphaz determine that Job lacked wisdom? Why did he warn Job that God judges the wicked? What does this tell us about Eliphaz's judgment of Job's faith?

From the Commentary

Job's response is to utter three heartfelt requests: first, a plea to his friends for sympathy (Job 16:1–14); then, a plea to God for justice (vv. 15–22); and finally, a plea to God to end his life and relieve him of suffering (17:1–16).

(1) A plea for sympathy (Job 16:1–14). Job's friends still had not identified with his situation; they did not feel his agony or understand his perplexity. Job had already called them deceitful brooks (see 6:15) and "worthless physicians" (13:4 NIV), but now he calls them "miserable comforters" (16:2). All of their attempts to comfort him only made him more miserable! As the saying goes, "With friends like you, who needs enemies?"

Job assured them that, if they were in his shoes, he would treat them with more understanding than they were showing him. Instead of making long speeches, he would give them words of encouragement. He would listen with his heart and try to help them bear their burdens. Sometimes we have to experience misunderstanding from unsympathetic friends in order to learn how to minister to others. This was a new experience for Job, and he was trying to make the most of it. However, whether Job spoke or kept quiet, he was still a suffering man (v. 6).

—*Be Patient*, pages 75–76

8. How did Job's friends end up acting more like enemies toward him? Why did Job tell his friends how he'd have responded were they in a similar situation? What would it have looked like for Job's friends to respond with understanding instead of judgment?

From the Commentary

Job was caught on the horns of a dilemma. His suffering was so great that he longed to die, but he didn't want to die before he could vindicate himself or see God vindicate him. This explains his cry in verse 18: "O earth, do not cover my blood, and let my cry have no resting place!" (NKJV). The ancients believed that the blood of innocent victims cried out to God for justice (Gen. 4:8–15) and that the spirits of the dead were restless until the corpses were properly buried (Isa. 26:21). Even if Job died, he would be restless until he had been proved righteous by the Lord.

—*Be Patient*, pages 76–77

9. Read Job 16:15–22. How had Job responded to Satan's attacks? Why did he say he wanted to die? What does this say about Job's faith? About his fears?

More to Consider: The Christian believer has a heavenly Advocate in Jesus Christ (1 John 2:1–2). How does Jesus help us when we are tempted and tested? (See Heb. 2:17–18; 4:14–16.) What happens when we fail (1 John 1:5—2:2)?

From the Commentary

> One reason Job wanted his heavenly Advocate to act quickly was because he sensed that death was very near, "the journey of no return" (Job 16:22 NIV). When people suffer so much that their "spirit is broken" (17:1 NIV, NASB), then they lose their "fight" and want life to end.
>
> Job's friends were against him and would not go to court and "post bond" for him (vv. 3–5). People treated Job as if he were the scum of the earth (v. 6). His body was only the shadow of what it had been (v. 7), and all of his plans had been shattered (v. 11). His friends would not change their minds and come to his defense (v. 10). In fact, they would not face his situation honestly, but they kept telling him that the light would soon dawn for him (v. 12). Is it any wonder that Job saw in death the only way of escape?
>
> —*Be Patient*, pages 77–78

10. Review Job 17:1–16. Why is it significant that Job didn't consider taking his own life? How is this different than asking God to take him? What did Job hope to accomplish by asking God to take his life?

Looking Inward

Take a moment to reflect on all that you've explored thus far in this study of Job 11—17. Review your notes and answers and think about how each of these things matters in your life today.

Tips for Small Groups: To get the most out of this section, form pairs or trios and have group members take turns answering these questions. Be honest and as open as you can in this discussion, but most of all, be encouraging and supportive of others. Be sensitive to those who are going through particularly difficult times and don't press for people to speak if they're uncomfortable doing so.

11. Have you ever been angry at God about suffering you thought you (or someone you cared for) didn't deserve? If so, how did you deal with your anger? If not, do you think such anger is wrong? Explain. How able are you to say honestly what Job said in 13:15?

12. Think about a time you judged someone for his or her actions. What led to your conclusions about that person? How did you (or didn't you) consider God's truth in that judgment? What did you do right? What could you have done better?

13. Have you ever wished that God would just take you? What prompted that feeling? How did you work through the sense of futility? Where can you turn when you feel like giving up?

Going Forward

14. Think of one or two things that you have learned that you'd like to work on in the coming week. Remember that this is all about quality, not quantity. It's better to work on one specific area of life and do it well than to work on many and do poorly (or to be so overwhelmed that you simply don't try).

Do you want to learn how to be less judgmental in your counsel of others? Be specific. Go back through Job 11—17 and put a star next to the phrase or verse that is most encouraging to you. Consider memorizing this verse.

Real-Life Application Ideas: Job's friends weren't really there for him in his greatest time of need. Instead, they spent all their time offering bad counsel. How might Job have dealt with his troubles if his friends had just been there for him, listening, offering encouragement, and generally being good friends? Put this idea of "being there" into practice this week by volunteering to spend time with someone who is suffering. Perhaps you can volunteer to help in a hospital or hospice. Or maybe you can deliver food and conversation to shut-ins.

Seeking Help

15. Write a prayer below (or simply pray one in silence), inviting God to work on your mind and heart in those areas you've noted above. Be honest about your desires and fears.

Notes for Small Groups:

- *Look for ways to put into practice the things you wrote in the Going Forward section. Talk with other group members about your ideas and commit to being accountable to one another.*

- *During the coming week, ask the Holy Spirit to continue to reveal truth to you from what you've read and studied.*

- *Before you start the next lesson, read Job 18—21. For more in-depth lesson preparation, read chapters 6 and 7, "Will the Real Enemy Please Stand Up?" and "It All Depends on Your Point of View," in* Be Patient.

The Real Enemy
(JOB 18—21)

Before you begin …
- *Pray for the Holy Spirit to reveal truth and wisdom as you go through this lesson.*
- *Read Job 18—21. This lesson references chapters 6 and 7 in* Be Patient. *It will be helpful for you to have your Bible and a copy of the commentary available as you work through this lesson.*

Getting Started

From the Commentary

Bildad opened his second speech with the same words he used in his first speech: "How long?" (Job 18:2; 8:2), and Job said the same thing when he replied (19:2). The friends were growing impatient with each other because their conversation seemed to be getting nowhere. George Bernard Shaw compared the average conversation to "a phonograph with half-a-dozen records—you soon get tired of them all."

Bildad blamed Job for the stalemate and admonished him, "Be sensible, and then we can talk" (18:2 NIV). It never dawned on Bildad that he and his two friends were playing the same tunes over and over again: (1) God is just; (2) God punishes the wicked and blesses the righteous; (3) since Job is suffering, he must be wicked; (4) if he turns from his sins, God will again bless him. They were going around in circles.

—*Be Patient*, page 85

1. Why did Bildad (and the other friends) keep harping on the same themes? Why did Bildad say Job wasn't being sensible or responsible? How did Bildad use sarcasm in his speech? What does this say about his patience with Job?

More to Consider: Bildad used fear as a motivator in his speech. How is this similar to the way fear is used to deliver a message of judgment in the New Testament? (See Matt. 10:28; 2 Cor. 5:11.) How is it different?

2. Choose one verse or phrase from Job 18—21 that stands out to you. This could be something you're intrigued by, something that makes you uncomfortable, something that puzzles you, something that resonates with you, or just something you want to examine further. Write that here.

Going Deeper

From the Commentary

In this address, Bildad painted four vivid pictures of the death of the wicked. Here are the first two:

(1) A light put out (Job 18:5–6). Light is associated with life just as darkness is associated with death. Since God is the author of life, He alone can "light our lamp"; for "He gives to all life, breath, and all things," and "in Him we live and move and have our being" (Acts 17:25, 28 NKJV). The picture here is that of a lamp hanging in a tent and a fire smoldering in a fire pot. Suddenly, the lamp goes out, and the last spark of the fire vanishes, and the tent is in total darkness (Prov. 13:9; 24:20).

(2) A traveler trapped (Job 18:7–10). Frightened, the man leaves his tent and starts down the road, looking for a place of safety. But the road turns out to be the most dangerous place of all, for it is punctuated by traps. Bildad used six words to describe the dangers people face when they try to run away from death:

a net—spread across the path to catch him

a snare—branches covering a deep pit

a trap—a "gin" (snare) with a noose that springs when touched; he is caught by the heel

a robber—another pitfall

a snare—a noose hidden on the ground

a trap—any device that catches prey

—*Be Patient*, page 87

3. Circle the words Bildad used to describe the dangers people face when they try to run away from death. (See Job 18:7–10.) Why would Bildad use such vivid pictures in his speech to Job? What was the purpose of being so blunt?

From the Commentary

Here are the second two pictures Bildad painted of the death of the wicked:

(3) A criminal pursued (Job 18:11–15). Death is "the king of terrors" (v. 14), determined to arrest the culprit no matter where he is. If the escaped criminal runs on the path and escapes the traps, then death will send some of his helpers to chase him. Terror frightens him, calamity eats away at his strength, and disaster waits for him to fall (vv. 11–12 NIV).

The frightened criminal gets weaker and weaker but still tries to keep going. If he goes back to his tent to hide, the pursuers find him, arrest him, drag him out, and take him to the king of terrors. They take everything out of his tent, burn the tent, and then scatter sulfur over the ashes. The end of that man is fire and brimstone!

(4) A tree rooted up (Job 18:16–21). Sometimes death is not as dramatic and sudden as the arresting of a criminal. Death may be gradual, like the dying of a tree. The roots dry up, the branches start to wither, and the dead branches are cut off one by one. Soon the tree is completely dead, and men chop it down. The death of a tree illustrates the extinction of a family, a "family tree." Not only is the wicked man himself cut down, but all the branches are cut down too; and he leaves no descendants to carry on his name. (Remember, all of Job's children had been

killed by the great wind.) In the East, the extinction of a
family was viewed as a great tragedy.

—*Be Patient*, page 88

4. Job used the tree as an illustration of resurrection (14:7–11). How did
Bildad use the tree to illustrate a different message (18:16–21)? How helpful
do you think it was to ask Job to meditate on death? Can you think of any
situations where it might be helpful for a person to reflect deeply on death?

From the Commentary

Bildad had given four frightening pictures of the terrors
of death, so Job countered with seven vivid pictures of
the trials of his life, what he was experiencing right then
and there!

1. He felt like *an animal trapped* (19:6).

2. He also felt like *a criminal in court* (19:7).

3. Job saw himself as *a traveler fenced in* (19:8).

4. Job's suffering left him feeling like *a king dethroned* (19:9).

5. His fifth picture is that of *a structure destroyed* (19:10).

6. In the sixth picture, Job borrowed the image of *a tree uprooted* (19:10; see 18:16).

7. Job's final picture is that of *a besieged city* (19:11–12).

—*Be Patient*, pages 89–91

5. Review Job 19:5–12. What was Job's response to Bildad? Why did he respond with seven illustrations? What was the message of each illustration?

From the Commentary

Job went on to explain how his suffering affected his relationship with people. We must recognize that extreme and prolonged pain often isolates sufferers from people and circumstances around them. When people really hurt, they may tend to withdraw and give the impression that others don't really understand what they are going through. Job felt alienated from those left in his family, from his friends, and even from his servants.

But there was more to this alienation than Job's pain. He was now bankrupt and ill, living at the city dump; and nobody wanted to be identified with him. Furthermore, people were convinced that Job was a guilty sinner suffering the judgment of God, so why be his friend? His appearance was repulsive, and people avoided looking at him. He was being treated like a leper, an outcast who was not wanted by family or friends.

Job's statement in Job 19:20 has become a familiar but misunderstood proverb: "I am escaped with the skin of my teeth." This is usually quoted, "I escaped *by* the skin of my teeth," that is, "I just barely escaped!" (If there were skin on our teeth, how thick would it be?) But the Hebrew text says "with" and not "by," and interpreters don't agree on the meaning.

—*Be Patient*, pages 91–92

6. What did Job mean that he escaped "with the skin of his teeth"? Why did he appeal for pity from his friends? What did Job want his friends to do?

From the Commentary

Zophar makes three affirmations to prove that the fate of the wicked is indeed terrible: their life is brief (Job 20:4–11), their pleasure is temporary (vv. 12–19), and their death is painful (vv. 20–29).

(1) Their life is brief (Job 20:4–11). Zophar declares that from the beginning of human history the triumphing ("mirth") of the wicked has been short. We wonder where he got his information, for the Lord waited 120 years before sending the flood (Gen. 6:3), and God gave the wicked Canaanites at least four centuries before He judged them (15:13–16).

(2) Their pleasure is temporary (Job 20:12–19). Zophar uses *eating* as his basic image here. The wicked man enjoys sin the way people enjoy food, keeping it in his mouth where he can "taste it" before swallowing it. In fact, he enjoys sin so much, he can't make himself swallow it! But eventually that delicious food in his mouth becomes poison in his system, and he becomes ill and vomits everything up.

(3) Their death is painful (Job 20:20–29). Not even his riches will be able to prevent death from coming to the wicked man (Job 20:20; see Ps. 49). While he is enjoying his prosperity, the wicked man will experience distress, misery, and God's burning anger. God will "rain down his blows upon him" (Job 20:23 NIV). The evil man will try to run away, but God will come at him with a sword and shoot at him with a bronze-tipped arrow that will pierce him.

—*Be Patient*, pages 97–100

7. Review Job 20:4–29. Why did Zophar continue the message about the fate of the wicked? Was he trying to frighten Job? Explain. What did his friends' persistence say about Job's stubbornness?

From the Commentary

After appealing once more for their understanding and sympathy (Job 21:1–6), Job replied to Zophar's statements and refuted each of them. Job stated that, from his point of view, it appears that the wicked have long lives (vv. 7–16), they are not often sent calamity (vv. 17–21), and the death of the wicked is no different from the death of other men (vv. 22–34). Point by point, Job took Zophar's speech and shredded it into bits.

But first, listen to Job's appeal to his friends that they try to understand how he feels. "If you really want to console me, just keep quiet and listen" (v. 2, paraphrase). The

Greek philosopher Zeno said, "The reason why we have two ears and only one mouth is that we may listen the more and talk the less." The friends thought their words would encourage Job, but he said that their silence would encourage him even more (13:3).

—*Be Patient*, pages 100–1

8. How did Job refute Zophar? Why did Job explain that his complaint isn't against man, but God? What had fueled Job's impatience with God? What was his appeal to his friends?

From the Commentary

In contrast to Zophar's text (20:5), Job said, "Why do the wicked still live, continue on, also become very powerful?" (21:7 NASB). They have security on every side: their children and homes are safe (vv. 8–9, 11–12), their businesses prosper (v. 10), and they have long lives in which to enjoy their prosperity (v. 13). They also have many descendants who share the family wealth and enjoy it. The death of the wicked is sudden; they don't linger in agony and long for deliverance. Of course, Job's situation was just the opposite: His family had been destroyed, his wealth was gone, and he was suffering greatly as he waited for death to come.

—Be Patient, page 101

9. Why did Job point out that the wicked live long lives? To what extent do you think his assessment of wicked people's lives is correct? Is God unfair when He lets a wicked person live a long, comfortable life? Explain.

More to Consider: Read Job 21:14–15. The philosophy of most unsaved people today might be called "practical atheism." (See Ps. 10.) God is not in their thoughts, let alone in their plans (James 4:13–17). How did Jesus describe these people (Luke 12:13–21)? Why?

From the Commentary

"Yea, the light of the wicked shall be put out," Bildad affirmed (18:5); but Job asked, "How often does that happen?" How often do you actually see God's anger displayed against the godless people of the world? "How often are they like straw before the wind, like chaff swept away by a gale?" (21:18 NIV). The wicked seem to be secure in this world, while the righteous suffer (but see Ps. 73).

But if God doesn't judge the wicked, He will judge their children (Job 21:19). Zophar had argued that point (20:10), and so had Eliphaz (5:4). Of course, both of them were aiming at Job, who had lost all of his children. "But what kind of judgment is that?" asked Job. "If a man lives in sin, let him suffer for his sin. After he dies, why should he care about what happens to his family? In Sheol, he will never know what is happening on earth."

—*Be Patient*, pages 102–3

10. Read Jeremiah 31:29–30 and Ezekiel 18:1–4. How do these verses support Job's claim that children aren't punished for the sins of their parents? Why was this important to Job's circumstance? How does Deuteronomy 24:16 speak to this issue?

Looking Inward

Take a moment to reflect on all that you've explored thus far in this study of Job 18—21. Review your notes and answers and think about how each of these things matters in your life today.

> *Tips for Small Groups: To get the most out of this section, form pairs or trios and have group members take turns answering these questions. Be honest and as open as you can in this discussion, but most of all, be encouraging and supportive of others. Be sensitive to those who are going through particularly difficult times and don't press for people to speak if they're uncomfortable doing so.*

11. Think about a time when you were suffering. How did that suffering affect your relationship with others? How did they respond to your situation? What did you want from your friends? What did they want from you? What can you learn from Job's circumstance to better relate to others when you're suffering (or they are)?

12. Have you used fear as a motivator for others (friends, employees, family members)? How did that work out? What might have been a better approach?

13. If you're a parent, have you ever wondered if your sins have damaged your children? How is Job's answer to his friends about this subject a comfort to you? What challenges does it present?

Going Forward

14. Think of one or two things that you have learned that you'd like to work on in the coming week. Remember that this is all about quality, not quantity. It's better to work on one specific area of life and do it well than to work on many and do poorly (or to be so overwhelmed that you simply don't try).

Do you want to respond better when people judge or accuse you? Be specific. Go back through Job 18—21 and put a star next to the phrase or verse that is most encouraging to you. Consider memorizing this verse.

Real-Life Application Ideas: The discussion in Job about the "sins of the fathers" is a good reminder that the relationship between parents and children is important, even if the sins of one don't directly impact the salvation of the other. If you're a parent, use this week to build your relationship with your children. Are there bad feelings that need to be resolved? Work through them. Are there behavioral issues that need to be addressed? Address them in love. If you aren't a parent, consider working on your relationship with your own parents.

Seeking Help

15. Write a prayer below (or simply pray one in silence), inviting God to work on your mind and heart in those areas you've noted above. Be honest about your desires and fears.

Notes for Small Groups:

- *Look for ways to put into practice the things you wrote in the Going Forward section. Talk with other group members about your ideas and commit to being accountable to one another.*

- *During the coming week, ask the Holy Spirit to continue to reveal truth to you from what you've read and studied.*

- *Before you start the next lesson, read Job 22—24. For more in-depth lesson preparation, read chapter 8, "Order in the Court!" in* Be Patient.

The Court
(JOB 22—24)

Before you begin ...
- *Pray for the Holy Spirit to reveal truth and wisdom as you go through this lesson.*
- *Read Job 22—24. This lesson references chapter 8 in* Be Patient. *It will be helpful for you to have your Bible and a copy of the commentary available as you work through this lesson.*

Getting Started

From the Commentary

What should have been an encouraging discussion among friends had become an angry and painful debate. Instead of trying to calm things down, Eliphaz assumed the office of prosecuting attorney and turned the debate into a trial. It was three against one as Job sat on the ash heap and listened to his friends lie about him. According to the Jewish Talmud, "The slanderous tongue kills three:

the slandered, the slanderer, and him who listens to the slander." At the ash heap in Uz, it was death all around!

—*Be Patient*, page 111

1. Why did the discussion turn into an angry debate? Why does this often happen between well-meaning friends? When is it appropriate to have intense discussions of faith, fate, or other theological issues, and when is it not appropriate? What are some good ground rules for such discussions?

2. Choose one verse or phrase from Job 22—24 that stands out to you. This could be something you're intrigued by, something that makes you uncomfortable, something that puzzles you, something that resonates with you, or just something you want to examine further. Write that here.

Going Deeper

From the Commentary

> Eliphaz can't resist shooting a sarcastic barb at Job. "Is it for your piety that he [God] rebukes you and brings charges against you?" (v. 4 NIV). Courts don't try people for their righteousness but for their lawlessness! Therefore, since God has sent terrible judgments upon Job, he must be guilty of sin. "Is not your wickedness great? Are not your sins endless?" (v. 5 NIV). But Eliphaz missed the point that Job had been making: "Why does God send the punishment *before He arrests me, reads the indictment, and conducts the trial?*" It all seemed unfair.
>
> Eliphaz first accused Job of the sin of *pride* (vv. 1–3). Job was acting as though his character and conduct were important to God and beneficial to Him in some way.
>
> —*Be Patient*, pages 111–12

3. Describe the God of Eliphaz's theology. How does this God relate to sinners? In what ways were Job's character and conduct important to the real God? How was God counting on these to silence Satan?

More to Consider: Read the following: 1 Thessalonians 4:1; Hebrews 11:5; Genesis 6:5–6; Psalm 37:23. What do these passages say about the value God places on His people's character? (See also Ps. 18:19; Isa. 63:9; Heb. 4:14–16.)

From the Commentary

Eliphaz clinched his first point with evidence anybody could see: Job was suffering great trials, which were the consequences of his many sins (Job 22:10–11). Why else would he be in darkness, danger, and the depths of suffering? This was the hand of God indicating that Job was a godless man.

—*Be Patient*, page 113

4. Why was Eliphaz so certain about the reason for Job's suffering? What might this say about Eliphaz's own spiritual condition or circumstance? How do people apply this same theology today? Is it good theology? Why or why not?

From Today's World

In Christian circles, it's not uncommon to attribute sudden (or not-so-sudden) healing to God's hand. While God doesn't heal everyone who's suffering, when someone is healed, they're quick to give the credit to God, sometimes offering the simple praise "God is good" in thankfulness. But when people suffer, far fewer are quick to give the credit (or blame) to God. A broken world, or Satan himself, is blamed for the suffering of good people.

5. Why does the church have little difficulty crediting God for healing and other good events in people's lives but not for the suffering or harder experiences people face? What does this say about the theology of the modern church? How is this like or unlike the way Job's friends viewed his circumstances?

From the Commentary

> Eliphaz calls Job a hypocrite, a statement that was made—
> or hinted at—more than once since the discussion began.
> "The hypocrite's hope shall perish," said Bildad (8:13).
> "For the congregation of hypocrites shall be desolate,"

said Eliphaz (15:34). And Zophar said, "The joy of the hypocrite [is] but for a moment" (20:5).

A hypocrite is not a person who fails to reach his desired spiritual goals, because all of us fail in one way or another. A hypocrite is a person who doesn't even try to reach any goals, *but he makes people think that he has.* His profession and his practice never meet. The Puritan preacher Stephen Charnock said, "It is a sad thing to be Christians at a supper, heathens in our shops, and devils in our closets."

—*Be Patient,* page 114

6. Review Job 22:12–20. What was Eliphaz's answer for Job's apparent hypocrisy (22:12–14)? Was Job a hypocrite? Why or why not? How does hypocrisy continue to negatively affect the church today?

From the Commentary

Eliphaz was sincere in his appeal to Job, just as Zophar was sincere when he asked Job to return to God (11:13–20). "Submit to God and be at peace with him; in this way prosperity will come to you" (22:21 NIV). The word translated "prosperity" means "good of every kind." Of course, a hypocrite should return to God, not just to get out of trouble and restore his or her fortunes, but to please and glorify God in the rebuilding of character and service.

—*Be Patient*, page 115

7. What does it mean to "submit to God"? (See James 4:1–10 and Job 22:22–27.) What does God promise to those who repent and return to Him? Do you think Job was failing to submit to God? Explain.

From the Commentary

Instead of arguing with his friends, or compromising his integrity by giving in to Eliphaz's appeal, Job ignores them completely and speaks to and about the Lord. Job has already made it clear that his dispute was not with men but with God, and he emphasizes this fact in his speech.

We may paraphrase Job 23:2, "My complaint today is bitter, and I have to keep a heavy hand on myself to keep from doing nothing but groaning." Job's three friends did not understand how much discipline Job needed just to be able to talk with them. Instead of giving in to his pain and doing nothing but groan, Job sought to master his pain and not give in to self-pity. The next time you visit somebody in pain, keep in mind that suffering drains a person's energy and makes great demands on his strength and patience.

Job was prepared to state his case, present his arguments, and let God give the verdict. Job was confident that, despite God's great power as a Lawgiver, he would win his case, for he was an upright man, and God could not condemn the upright in heart. "There an upright man could present his case before him, and I would be delivered forever from my judge" (v. 7 NIV).

—*Be Patient*, page 116

8. Was it right for Job to ignore his friends and go right to God? Explain. How did Job go about pursuing God? What can Job teach us about how we're to pursue God and truth today?

More to Consider: Read Isaiah 48:10; Deuteronomy 4:20; Psalm 66:10; and 1 Peter 1:6–7. How does each of these passages use the image of a furnace to describe God's ministry through suffering?

From the Commentary

"But he stands alone, and who can oppose him? He does whatever he pleases" (v. 13 NIV). Job had no other gods to turn to for help, and no way to oppose God or change His mind. God runs the universe by decree, not by consensus or democratic vote. His thoughts and ways are far above ours, but He knows what is best, and we must accept His will and rejoice in it (Isa. 55:8–11).

Those who resist or deny the sovereignty of God rob themselves of peace and courage. "There is no attribute of God more comforting to His children than the doctrine of divine sovereignty," said Charles Haddon Spurgeon. "On the other hand, there is no doctrine more hated by worldlings." Why? Because the human heart is proud and does not want to submit to Almighty God. People want to do their own thing and do it their way, rather than find delight in doing the will of God.

—*Be Patient*, page 118

9. Review Job 23:1–17. How does pride get in the way of our relationship with God? Why was Job so frightened when he thought about the

sovereignty of God? What is the difference between being frightened about God's sovereignty and fearing God Himself?

From the Commentary

Job 24 focuses on the seeming injustices that God permits in this world. Job opens his speech by asking in effect, "Why doesn't God have specific days to hold court? Then I could attend and tell Him what I think of the way He is running the world!"

Job starts with *injustices in the country* (vv. 1–11), and then moves to *crimes in the city* (vv. 12–17). He closes his speech with *a curse on the wicked* (vv. 18–25). If God won't judge them, Job will!

Job is to be commended for seeing somebody else's troubles besides his own and for expressing a holy anger against sin and injustice. Too often, personal suffering can make us selfish and even blind us to the needs of others, but Job was concerned that God help others who were hurting. His three friends were treating the problem of suffering in far too abstract a fashion, and Job tried to get them to see *hurting people* and not just philosophical problems. Jesus had the same problem with the Jewish lawyer who wanted to discuss "neighborliness," but not discover who his neighbor was and then try to help him (Luke 10:25–37).

—*Be Patient*, pages 119–21

10. How are Job's questions in chapter 24 similar to questions people have today about injustice? Why is it significant that he doesn't focus solely on his own circumstance here? What message does this give us today about how to respond to injustice?

Looking Inward

Take a moment to reflect on all that you've explored thus far in this study of Job 22—24. Review your notes and answers and think about how each of these things matters in your life today.

Tips for Small Groups: To get the most out of this section, form pairs or trios and have group members take turns answering these questions. Be honest and as open as you can in this discussion, but most of all, be encouraging and supportive of others. Be sensitive to those who are going through particularly difficult times and don't press for people to speak if they're uncomfortable doing so.

11. Have you ever been "ganged up on" by friends who meant well but ended up making you feel worse? Describe the circumstance. What role did your relationship with God play in that story? How do you stand strong in your faith when others challenge you?

12. Do you attribute the good things that happen in your life to God's hand? Why or why not? How about the difficult things you endure? What active role does God play in your life? How does the way you view God's participation in your daily life affect the way you live out your faith?

13. Have you ever experienced injustice? If so, what was it like? What role did your faith play in that story? What do you do today when you observe injustice? How can your trust in God help you know how to respond?

Going Forward

14. Think of one or two things that you have learned that you'd like to work on in the coming week. Remember that this is all about quality, not quantity. It's better to work on one specific area of life and do it well than to work on many and do poorly (or to be so overwhelmed that you simply don't try).

Do you want to better understand the difference between being frightened of God and having an appropriate fear of God? Be specific. Go back through Job 22—24 and put a star next to the phrase or verse that is most encouraging to you. Consider memorizing this verse.

Real-Life Application Ideas: Study what God has to say about injustice. Then decide on practical actions you can take to challenge those injustices in a biblical way. Perhaps you can volunteer at a women's shelter or raise money to help war-torn countries rebuild. God hates injustice and will one day judge the world for all its sins, but while we are on earth, He can use each one of us to face injustice head-on, making a positive impact on the lives of others in His name.

Seeking Help

15. Write a prayer below (or simply pray one in silence), inviting God to work on your mind and heart in those areas you've noted above. Be honest about your desires and fears.

Notes for Small Groups:

- *Look for ways to put into practice the things you wrote in the Going Forward section. Talk with other group members about your ideas and commit to being accountable to one another.*

- *During the coming week, ask the Holy Spirit to continue to reveal truth to you from what you've read and studied.*

- *Before you start the next lesson, read Job 25—31. For more in-depth lesson preparation, read chapters 9 and 10, "How Faint a Whisper!" and "I Rest My Case!" in* Be Patient.

A Whisper
(JOB 25—31)

Before you begin ...
- *Pray for the Holy Spirit to reveal truth and wisdom as you go through this lesson.*
- *Read Job 25—31. This lesson references chapters 9 and 10 in* Be Patient. *It will be helpful for you to have your Bible and a copy of the commentary available as you work through this lesson.*

Getting Started

From the Commentary

Before magnifying God's great power in the universe, Job first rebuked Bildad for giving him no help (Job 26:1–4). Job had no power, but Bildad didn't make him stronger. According to his friends, Job lacked wisdom; yet Bildad didn't share one piece of wisdom or insight. "Who has helped you utter these words? And whose spirit spoke from your mouth?" (v. 4 NIV). If Bildad's words had come from God, then they would have done Job good; for Job had been crying out for God to speak to him. The conclusion is that Bildad's words came from Bildad, and that's why they did Job no good.

—*Be Patient*, page 126

1. Why did Job rebuke Bildad before extolling God's greatness? What were some of the ways Job acknowledged God's power in chapter 26? What do these descriptions tell us about God? About Job's understanding of God?

More to Consider: Respond to the following statement: The more we learn about God, the more we discover how much more there is to know! How does Job's story support this idea?

2. Choose one verse or phrase from Job 25—31 that stands out to you. This could be something you're intrigued by, something that makes you uncomfortable, something that puzzles you, something that resonates with you, or just something you want to examine further. Write that here.

Going Deeper

From the Commentary

> Job stood fast in affirming his integrity (10:1–7; 13:13–19; 19:23–27; 23:2–7); but this time, he gave an oath: "As God lives" (27:2). Among Eastern people in that day, taking an oath was a serious matter. It was like inviting God to kill you if what you said was not true. Job was so sure of himself that he was willing to take that chance.
>
> Job also repeated his charge that God was not treating him fairly ("[He] has denied me justice," v. 2 NIV). Job had asked God to declare the charges against him, but the heavens had been silent. Job had called for an umpire to bring him and God together, but no umpire had been provided.
>
> So Job declared that, as long as he lived, he would defend himself and maintain his integrity. He would not lie just to please his friends or to "bribe" God into restoring his fortunes. (Satan would have rejoiced at that!) Job had to live with his conscience ("heart," v. 6) no matter what his friends said or his God did to him.
>
> —*Be Patient*, pages 127–28

3. Why is it significant that Job took an oath? In what ways does Job's repeated declaration to defend his integrity define his character? What do you think Job was feeling as he continued to maintain his integrity?

From the Commentary

"I will teach you about the power of God" (27:11 NIV), says Job; and he describes God's judgment of the wicked. On the day when God vindicates Job, this is what will happen to his enemies.

They will die, and their widows will not mourn for them, a terrible insult in the Eastern world. Their children will be slain by the sword or the plague; and if any survive, they will spend the rest of their lives begging for something to eat. The wicked will lie down rich and wake up poor. Their silver and expensive clothing will be gone. Their houses will be destroyed like cocoons (or spiders' webs), or like the temporary shacks of the watchmen in the fields. The death of the wicked will not be peaceful. Terrors will come in at night like a flood and carry them away. Even if the wicked try to flee, the storm will follow them and destroy them.

—*Be Patient*, page 129

4. Review Job 27:11–23. How is Job's description of the wicked similar to what his friends told him? Why did he choose to use similar imagery? (See Matt. 7:1–2.)

From the Commentary

"But where shall wisdom be found?" (Job 28:12). "Where then does wisdom come from? Where does understanding dwell?" (v. 20 NIV). Job asked these questions because he was weary of the cliches and platitudes that his three friends were giving him in the name of "wisdom." His friends were sure that their words were pure gold, but Job concluded they were tinsel and trash. The three men had *knowledge*, but they lacked *wisdom*.

"Wisdom is the right use of knowledge," said Charles Spurgeon. "To know is not to be wise. Many men know a great deal, and are all the greater fools for it. There is no fool so great a fool as the knowing fool. But to know how to use knowledge is to have wisdom."

—*Be Patient*, page 130

5. What answers did Job give (in chapter 28) to his question "Where is wisdom found?" How was this a response to his friends? What does it tell us about Job's understanding of God?

From the Commentary

Job and his friends had shared three rounds of speeches, and now Job felt it was time for him to sum up his defense. The phrase "Moreover Job continued his parable [discourse]" (Job 29:1) suggests that Job may have paused and waited for Zophar to take his turn to speak, but Zophar was silent. Perhaps Zophar felt it was a waste of time to argue with Job anymore.

In chapters 29—31, Job *recalled the blessings of the past* (Job 29), *lamented the sufferings of the present* (Job 30), and *challenged God to vindicate him in the future* (Job 31). He climaxed his speech with sixteen "if I have ..." statements and put himself under oath, challenging God either to condemn him or vindicate him. It was as though Job were saying, "We've talked long enough! I really don't care what you three men think, because God is my Judge; and I rest my case with Him. Now, let Him settle the matter one way or another, once and for all."

—*Be Patient*, page 137

6. Why did Job include a recollection of his blessings in his defense (Job 29)? What was the purpose of Job's "If I have ..." statements? What do they reveal about Job's frustration? His hope?

From the Commentary

Job had opened his defense by saying that he wished he had never been born (Job 3). Now he closed his defense by remembering the blessings he and his family had enjoyed prior to his crisis. This is a good reminder that we should try to see life in a balanced way. Yes, God permits us to experience difficulties and sorrows, but God also sends victories and joys. "Shall we receive good at the hand of God, and shall we not receive evil?" (2:10). C. H. Spurgeon said that too many people write their blessings in the sand but engrave their sorrows in marble.

"Oh, that I were as in months past, as in the days when God preserved me" (29:2). When we are experiencing trials, it's natural for us to long for "the good old days"; but our longing will not change our situation. Someone has defined "the good old days" as "a combination of a bad memory and a good imagination." In Job's case, however, his memory was accurate, and "the good old days" really were good.

—*Be Patient*, pages 137–38

7. Why was it important for Job to remember the good from his past? How can remembering the past benefit us? (See Ps. 77:10–11.) What are the dangers of focusing solely on the past?

From the Commentary

From the delightful past, Job is suddenly thrust back into the dismal and disappointing present. You can almost hear him groan his first words, "But now" (Job 30:1; see vv. 9, 16). Job was wise enough to know that he had to face the reality of the present and not escape into the memory of the past. People who refuse to come to grips with life are in danger of losing touch with reality, and soon they lose touch with themselves.

"In their unsuccessful effort to fulfill their needs, no matter what behavior they choose," writes psychiatrist William Glasser, "all patients have a common characteristic: *They all deny the reality of the world around them*" (*Reality Therapy*, 6). By refusing to live in the past and by honestly facing reality, Job took a giant step in maturity and integrity. In his lament, Job contrasted his present situation with the past and showed how everything had been changed by the judgment of God. His five "complaints" parallel the joys that he named in chapter 29.

—*Be Patient*, pages 140–41

8. What are the five complaints Job described in chapter 30? How do they parallel the joys he named in chapter 29? Why was it important for Job to admit his current circumstances?

From the Commentary

> Chapter 31 records Job's final defense. It is like a legal document in which Job puts himself under oath before God and asks for judgment to fall if God can prove him wrong (Job 31:35–37). Job's only hope was that God would hear his cry and vindicate his name. He could die in peace if he knew that his enemies had been silenced and his reputation restored. In sixteen "if I have ..." statements, Job reviews his life and relationships and asks God to pass judgment. "I sign now my defense" (v. 35 NIV), said Job as he made the oath official and signed the document. "I rest my case!"

> —*Be Patient*, page 144

9. What did Job ask God for in 31:33–37? Why did he ask for these things? What does 31:33–34 tell us about Job's character?

From the Commentary

> Review Job's oath in chapter 31 and you will discover that he has asked God to send some terrible judgments if he is guilty of any of these sins: others will eat his harvest and uproot his crops (v. 8); his wife will become another man's servant and mistress (v. 10); his arm will fall from his shoulder (v. 22); his harvest will be weeds and thistles (v. 40). He made it clear that he was willing to face the righteous judgment of God (vv. 14, 23, 28) along with these other judgments.
>
> When the words of Job were ended, everybody sat in silence, wondering what would happen next. Would God send immediate judgment and prove Job guilty? Or would He accept Job's challenge, appear to him, and give Job opportunity to defend himself? Perhaps God would speak from heaven and answer Job's questions.
>
> Job had challenged God because he was sure God would vindicate him. Job's three friends were sure that God would condemn him.
>
> *—Be Patient*, page 147

10. Why did Job invite such terrible judgments upon himself if proven guilty? What must it have been like to sit in silence, awaiting God's judgment? What role does trust play in Job's story?

Looking Inward

Take a moment to reflect on all that you've explored thus far in this study of Job 25—31. Review your notes and answers and think about how each of these things matters in your life today.

Tips for Small Groups: To get the most out of this section, form pairs or trios and have group members take turns answering these questions. Be honest and as open as you can in this discussion, but most of all, be encouraging and supportive of others. Be sensitive to those who are going through particularly difficult times and don't press for people to speak if they're uncomfortable doing so.

11. Job fought to protect his integrity. Have you ever had your integrity challenged? What was that experience like? What are some of the main areas in which you make an effort to maintain your integrity?

12. Where do you find wisdom? Do you pursue wisdom intentionally? Why or why not? How can the pursuit of wisdom help you grow closer to Christ?

13. Job made his case and then waited on God for His answer. What are some things you're waiting on God for? What makes the waiting difficult? What makes it worthwhile?

Going Forward

14. Think of one or two things that you have learned that you'd like to work on in the coming week. Remember that this is all about quality, not quantity. It's better to work on one specific area of life and do it well than to work on many and do poorly (or to be so overwhelmed that you simply don't try).

Do you want to wait on God with more trust? Be specific. Go back through Job 25—31 and put a star next to the phrase or verse that is most encouraging to you. Consider memorizing this verse.

Real-Life Application Ideas: Job made a point to remember the good things from his past, not to linger in it, but to acknowledge God's role in shaping his life. Take a few minutes to recall the ways God has grown and shaped you in the past. Then thank God in prayer for all the good that He has granted you, and ask Him to continue to lead you today and into the future.

Seeking Help

15. Write a prayer below (or simply pray one in silence), inviting God to work on your mind and heart in those areas you've noted above. Be honest about your desires and fears.

Notes for Small Groups:

- *Look for ways to put into practice the things you wrote in the Going Forward section. Talk with other group members about your ideas and commit to being accountable to one another.*

- *During the coming week, ask the Holy Spirit to continue to reveal truth to you from what you've read and studied.*

- *Before you start the next lesson, read Job 32—37. For more in-depth lesson preparation, read chapters 11 and 12, "Elihu Has the Answers" and "Elihu Explains and Defends God," in* Be Patient.

Elihu's Defense
(JOB 32—37)

Before you begin ...
- *Pray for the Holy Spirit to reveal truth and wisdom as you go through this lesson.*
- *Read Job 32—37. This lesson references chapters 11 and 12 in* Be Patient. *It will be helpful for you to have your Bible and a copy of the commentary available as you work through this lesson.*

Getting Started

From the Commentary

Elihu gave a long speech—six chapters in our Bible—in which he explained the character of God and applied this truth to Job's situation. One way to outline his speech is as follows:

1. God is speaking through me (Job 32; note v. 8).

2. God is gracious (Job 33; note v. 24).

3. God is just (Job 34—35; note 34:10–12).

4. God is great (Job 36—37; note 36:5, 26).

—*Be Patient*, page 152

1. What new idea did Elihu introduce into the debate over Job's circumstances (Job 33:18, 24; 36:1–15)? Read 2 Corinthians 12:7–10 and Hebrews 12:1–11. How do these passages support the truths Elihu brought to the conversation? Why were they important for Job to hear? Why are they important for us to hear today?

2. Choose one verse or phrase from Job 32—37 that stands out to you. This could be something you're intrigued by, something that makes you uncomfortable, something that puzzles you, something that resonates with you, or just something you want to examine further. Write that here.

Going Deeper

From the Commentary

Elihu emphasized that he had waited patiently before speaking, and he gave two reasons. For one thing, he was younger than Job and the three friends; and youth must respect age and experience (Job 32:4, 6–7). It would have been a terrible breach of etiquette had Elihu interrupted his elders.

His second reason was because he wanted to hear the complete debate and have all the arguments before him (v. 11; Prov. 18:13).… Like many "young theologians," Elihu had a bit of youthful conceit in his speeches ("Hear what I know!"—vv. 6, 10, 17; 33:1–3); but for the most part, he was a sincere young man who really thought he could help Job find answers to his questions.

—*Be Patient*, pages 152–53

3. Elihu quoted from the others' speeches. What does this tell us about him? What evidence do we have in Elihu's speech of his sincerity?

More to Consider: Read Proverbs 16:31. How does this truth apply to Elihu's situation? What claims did Elihu present that made his youth unimportant in this story?

From the Commentary

Job 33 is a remarkable speech because it introduces into the debate a new insight into the purpose of suffering. Job's friends had argued that his suffering was evidence that God was punishing him for his sins, but Elihu now argues that sometimes God permits us to suffer *to keep us from sin.* In other words, suffering may be *preventive* and not *punitive.* (See Paul's experience recorded in 2 Cor. 12:7–10.) God does all He can to keep us from sinning and going into the pit of death, and this is evidence of His grace (Job 33:24).

Before launching into his argument, Elihu assured Job that his words were sincere and given by God's Spirit, so Job had no reason to be afraid (vv. 1–7). Elihu didn't claim to have any "inside track" with God; he was made of clay just like Job. He promised not to be heavy-handed in his speaking, and he invited Job to feel free to reply. Elihu didn't want this to be a monologue, but that's exactly what it turned out to be. Either Job was silenced by what Elihu said, or Elihu didn't pause long enough for Job to speak (see vv. 31, 33), or Job didn't think it was worthwhile to respond.

—Be Patient, page 155

4. Why is it important to note that the purpose of suffering might be preventive instead of punitive? How might Job's friends have received this? What does this reveal about the character of God?

From the Commentary

> In *The Problem of Pain*, C. S. Lewis says, "God whispers to us in our pleasures, speaks in our conscience, but shouts in our pains: It is His megaphone to rouse a deaf world." God sometimes uses pain to warn us, humble us, and bring us to the place of submission (Heb. 12:1–11). Elihu describes a sick man, suffering on his bed, wasting away because he has no appetite. (Is this a picture of Job? See 6:7; 7:3–6; 16:8; 17:7; 19:20.) But this man is suffering because God wants to get his attention and prevent him from breaking God's law.
>
> —*Be Patient*, page 157

5. Review Job 33:19–22. Why would it be wrong to claim that all suffering is punishment for sin? Describe some examples to support this. Read

Hebrews 11:25 and 1 Peter 4:12–13. How do these verses shed light on this issue?

From the Commentary

> Elihu had promised not to use flattery (Job 32:21), but he came close to it in 34:2 when he addressed his audience as "wise men" and "men of learning" (NIV). Actually, he was flattering himself; because if these "learned wise men" were willing to listen to him, they must have thought that he was more learned and wise than they! Quoting Job's words (v. 3; 12:11), Elihu urged them to use discernment as they "tasted" his words, so that he and they might "learn together what is good" (34:4 NIV). Elihu compared his speaking to the enjoyment of a tasteful and nourishing meal.
>
> —*Be Patient*, page 164

6. What complaints of Job's did Elihu discuss (34:5–6, 7–9)? What were Elihu's answers to those complaints (34:10–37; 35)? How did Elihu's confidence affect the message?

From the Commentary

> One of Job's complaints was that God was silent and
> had hidden His face from him (9:11; 23:1–9), but Elihu
> had an answer for that: "But if He remains silent, who
> can condemn him? If he hides his face, who can see
> him?" (34:29 NIV). In Job 24, Job had accused God of
> ignoring men's sins, but what right had he to judge the
> Judge?
>
> —Be Patient, page 166

7. In Genesis 15:13–16, God predicted that Abraham's descendants would
be slaves in Egypt for four hundred years before God delivered them. What
does that tell us about God's silence? How does 2 Peter 3:9 support Elihu's
argument about God's silence?

From the Commentary

> Having disposed of Job's first complaint, Elihu turns to
> the second one: "There is no profit in obeying God" (Job
> 34:7–9; 35:1–16).

Again, Elihu tries to throw Job's own words back in his face: "I am innocent" (10:7; 12:4; 27:6), and "What have I gained by obeying God?" (9:29–31; 21:15). Job did make the first statement, but the second is not an accurate quotation of his words. *Job never did bargain with God as Satan said he would* (1:9, 21; 2:9–10). Eliphaz had discussed this topic (Job 22) and had come to the conclusion that neither man's piety nor his iniquity could make any difference to the character of God. But Elihu felt it was important to deal with the theme again.

Elihu asked his listeners to look up to the heavens and see how far away the clouds were, and then imagine how far God's throne was from the earth (35:5–7). Can a man's sins or good deeds on earth exert such power that they will travel all that distance and change the Almighty in heaven?

Then Elihu asked them to consider human society (vv. 8–16). Our sins or good works may affect people around us (v. 8), but God is not affected by them. Certainly God grieves over man's sins (Gen. 6:6) and delights in the obedience of the faithful (Ps. 37:23); but our good deeds can't bribe Him, and our misdeeds can't threaten Him. God's character is the same whether men obey Him or disobey Him. God can't change for the better because He is perfect, and He can't change for the worse because He is holy.

—*Be Patient*, page 167

8. Respond to this question that Elihu presented: Can a man's sins or good deeds on earth exert such power that they will change the Almighty

in heaven? How does Elihu's argument answer Job's complaint? How do people today sometimes challenge God's unchangeable nature in word or deed? Does this mean God doesn't respond to our pleas? Explain.

From the Commentary

> Elihu's self-importance reaches new heights as he introduces the last third of his speech (36:1–4). His listeners must have been getting restless; otherwise, why did he have to say, "Bear with me a little [longer]" (v. 2 NIV)? The statement "I will fetch my knowledge from afar" (v. 3) suggests that either he is boasting of wide knowledge or of getting his knowledge right from heaven. And to call himself "one perfect in knowledge" (v. 4 NIV) is hardly an evidence of humility!
>
> —*Be Patient*, pages 168–69

9. When did Elihu's confidence slide into arrogance? How was Elihu's approach ultimately similar to that of Job's other friends? How did Elihu try to separate himself from them? In what way is Elihu's arrogance similar to some church leaders' today?

More to Consider: Job thought that God was ignoring him. How do the following verses answer that concern: Job 36:7; 1 Peter 3:12; Luke 1:52–53?

From the Commentary

"Behold, God is great, and we know him not" (Job 36:26). This is the theme of the last part of Elihu's speech; and he illustrated it with the works of God in nature, specifically, God's control of His world during the seasons of the year.

Elihu's closing words remind us that, even though we can't fully understand God, we know that He is great and just and does not afflict men to no purpose. What should our personal response be? "Therefore, fear him!" Job had come to that same conclusion after pondering the works of God in the world (Job 28:24–28).

—*Be Patient*, pages 171, 173

10. How did Elihu use each of the seasons to describe God's power in Job 36:26—37:24? What do Elihu's closing comments reveal about God? About Elihu himself? About Job's circumstances?

Looking Inward

Take a moment to reflect on all that you've explored thus far in this study of Job 32—37. Review your notes and answers and think about how each of these things matters in your life today.

> *Tips for Small Groups: To get the most out of this section, form pairs or trios and have group members take turns answering these questions. Be honest and as open as you can in this discussion, but most of all, be encouraging and supportive of others. Be sensitive to those who are going through particularly difficult times and don't press for people to speak if they're uncomfortable doing so.*

11. What wisdom did you acquire as a young person? What wisdom have you acquired as an adult? Do you believe wisdom can only come with age? Why or why not? What are some examples of truth you've learned from the young?

12. Have you ever felt like God was punishing you? Describe one of those times. How might God have been using your suffering to prevent sin, or for some other reason, rather than punishing you for it?

13. Elihu talked about the unknowable nature of God. What are some of the things that help you see God's greatness? How does that affect the way you live out your faith? Does God's greatness overwhelm you? Frighten you? Comfort you? Explain.

Going Forward

14. Think of one or two things that you have learned that you'd like to work on in the coming week. Remember that this is all about quality, not quantity. It's better to work on one specific area of life and do it well than to work on many and do poorly (or to be so overwhelmed that you simply don't try).

Do you want to learn how to speak confidently about your faith, but not arrogantly? Be specific. Go back through Job 32—37 and put a star next to the phrase or verse that is most encouraging to you. Consider memorizing this verse.

Real-Life Application Ideas: Elihu may have been arrogant in his speeches, but his claim that he had some wisdom from God wasn't totally unfounded. Take time this week to consider the wisdom of the young. Track down young leaders in the church and study what they have to offer. Then test it against the wisdom you've gained from older, more seasoned teachers and leaders.

Seeking Help

15. Write a prayer below (or simply pray one in silence), inviting God to work on your mind and heart in those areas you've noted above. Be honest about your desires and fears.

Notes for Small Groups:

- *Look for ways to put into practice the things you wrote in the Going Forward section. Talk with other group members about your ideas and commit to being accountable to one another.*

- *During the coming week, ask the Holy Spirit to continue to reveal truth to you from what you've read and studied.*

- *Before you start the next lesson, read Job 38—42. For more in-depth lesson preparation, read chapter 13, "The Final Examination," in* Be Patient.

The Final Examination

(JOB 38—42)

Before you begin …
- *Pray for the Holy Spirit to reveal truth and wisdom as you go through this lesson.*
- *Read Job 38—42. This lesson references chapter 13 in* Be Patient. *It will be helpful for you to have your Bible and a copy of the commentary available as you work through this lesson.*

Getting Started

From the Commentary

With all his verbosity and lack of humility, Elihu did say some good things that Job needed to hear. Elihu's use of rhetorical questions in Job 37:14–18 prepared Job for the series of questions Jehovah would ask him in Job 38—41. Unlike the three friends, Elihu assessed Job's problem accurately: Job's *actions* may have been right—he was not the sinner his three friends described him to be—but his *attitude* was wrong. He was not the "saint" Job saw himself to be. Job was slowly moving toward a defiant, self-righteous attitude that was not at all healthy. It was this know-it-all attitude that God exposed and destroyed when He appeared to Job and questioned him.

—*Be Patient*, page 177

1. What was the most valuable thing Elihu said in his speech to Job? Why did Job not want to accept what Elihu said? What does Elihu's role in this story teach us about one of the ways God reveals Himself to us?

2. Choose one verse or phrase from Job 38—42 that stands out to you. This could be something you're intrigued by, something that makes you uncomfortable, something that puzzles you, something that resonates with you, or just something you want to examine further. Write that here.

Going Deeper

From the Commentary

> The storm that Elihu had been describing finally broke, and God spoke to Job out of the storm. The answer to Job's problems was not an *explanation about God*, such as the three friends and Elihu had given, but a *revelation of God*. The four men had declared and defended the greatness of God but had failed to persuade Job. When God displayed His majesty and greatness, it humbled Job and brought him to the place of silent submission before God. That was the turning point.
>
> —*Be Patient*, page 179

3. What's the difference between an explanation of God and a revelation of God? Why were Job's friends destined to fail in their approach to Job? How did God finally speak to Job?

More to Consider: Dr. Paul Tournier wrote in his book Guilt and Grace, *"For God's answer is not an idea, a proposition, like the conclusion of a theorem; it is Himself. He revealed Himself to Job; Job found personal contact with God" (86). How is this evident in Job's story? What are other biblical stories where this proves to be true? How is it true for believers today?*

From the Commentary

God's address to Job centered on His works in nature and consisted of seventy-seven questions interspersed with divine commentary relating to the questions. The whole purpose of this interrogation was to make Job realize his own inadequacy and inability to meet God *as an equal* and defend his cause.

"Then summon me, and I will answer," Job had challenged God, "or let me speak, and you reply" (Job 13:22 NIV). God had now responded to Job's challenge.

God's address can be summarized in three questions:

1. "Can you explain My creation?" (38:1–38).

2. "Can you oversee My creation?" (38:39—39:30).

3. "Can you subdue My creation?" (40:6—41:34).

—*Be Patient*, page 180

4. What was the tone of God's reply to Job? Why did God focus His address on the subject of creation? How did this answer Job's complaints?

From the Commentary

Job was sure that his speeches had been filled with wisdom and knowledge, but God's first question put an end to that delusion: "Who is this that darkens my counsel with words without knowledge?" (Job 38:2 NIV). The Living Bible paraphrases it, "Why are you using your ignorance to deny my providence?" God didn't question Job's integrity or sincerity; He only questioned Job's ability to explain the ways of God in the world. Job had spoken the truth about God (42:7), but his speeches had lacked humility. Job thought he knew about God, but he didn't realize how much he *didn't* know about God. Knowledge of our own ignorance is the first step toward true wisdom.

—*Be Patient*, page 181

5. Review Job 38:1–38. How did Job use his ignorance to deny God's providence? What does this passage teach us about the dangers of an arrogant faith? How might the church today benefit from the lesson God gave Job?

From the Commentary

The question "Canst thou set its dominion thereof in the earth?" (Job 38:33) is translated in the NASB, "Or fix their rule over the earth?" The NIV reads, "Can you set up God's dominion over the earth?" and The Living Bible says, "Do you know … how the heavens influence the earth?" Is there a suggestion here that the stars and planets have a direct influence over events on earth as the advocates of astrology maintain? Not at all. The statement can be paraphrased: "Job, if you understand so much about the heavenly bodies that are thought by some to affect the earth, then why don't you use that authority to change your situation?" The Lord was speaking with "holy sarcasm" and not revealing some profound truth.

—*Be Patient*, page 183

6. What's the point of God's "holy sarcasm" in his response to Job? What does this suggest about Job's stubbornness? About God's perspective on Job's attitude?

From the Commentary

The Lord brought before Job's imagination a parade of six beasts (lioness, goat, hind [deer], wild donkey, wild ox, and horse) and five birds (raven, ostrich, stork, hawk, and eagle). As he contemplated these creatures, Job had to answer the question, "Do you understand how they live and how to take care of them?" Obviously, Job's reply had to be no.

The providence of God is certainly remarkable (see Ps. 104). In His wisdom and power, God supervises the whole universe and makes sure that His creatures are cared for. "You open Your hand and satisfy the desire of every living thing" (Ps. 145:16 NKJV). We humans have a difficult time keeping the machinery of life operating successfully, but God runs the whole universe with such precision that we build our scientific laws on His creation.

Did Job know how to feed the lion cubs or the young ravens (Job 38:39–41)? Would he even know that they were hungry? Where could he find food for them? The ravens would know to find the carcasses left behind by the lions because God taught the birds (even unclean ravens!) how to find food.

—*Be Patient*, pages 183–84

7. Why did God refer to creatures of the earth in His answer to Job? How might that have connected with Job better than theoretical argument? What do God's words here teach us about His creativity, both in creation

and in answering people's questions? How can the church today learn from God's speech?

From the Commentary

> God uses language that reflected Job's desire to take God to court and argue his case. "Will the faultfinder contend with the Almighty? Let him who reproves God answer it" (Job 40:2 NASB). God presented His case; now He gave Job opportunity to present his case. But Job has no case to present! His first words were, "Behold, I am vile!" which means, "I am insignificant and unworthy. I have no right to debate with God." Job had told his friends to cover their mouths (21:5), and others had covered their mouths when Job appeared (29:9); but now Job had to put his hand over his mouth lest he say something he shouldn't say (Prov. 30:32; Rom. 3:19).

> But Job was not quite broken and at the place of sincere repentance. He was silent but not yet submissive; so, God continued His address.

> —*Be Patient*, pages 185–86

8. How do you think Job felt when God silenced him in this way? Why is it critical for us to be silenced by God before He can accomplish His will? What does it mean to be silent but not submissive? How is this true sometimes in the church today?

From the Commentary

> Instead of confronting Job again with the broad sweep of His creation, God selected only two creatures and asked Job to consider them. It's as though God were saying, "My whole universe is too much for you to handle. However, here are two of My best products. What can you do with them?"
>
> The issue now is not the *power* of God but the *justice* of God (Job 40:8). Job had said that God was unjust in the way He treated him (6:29; 27:1–6) and in the way He failed to judge the wicked (21:29–31; 24:1–17). In 40:9–14, God asked, "Job, do you have the strength and holy wrath it takes to judge sinners? If so, then start judging them! Humble the proud sinners and crush the wicked! Bury them! You claim that you can do a better job than I can of bringing justice to the world, so I'll let you do it!"

However, before God turned Job loose on the sinners of the world, He asked him to put on his majestic robes and "practice" on two of His finest creatures, the hippopotamus (vv. 15–24) and the crocodile (41:1–34). If Job succeeded in subduing them, then he would qualify to execute judgment against a sinful world.

—*Be Patient*, page 186

9. Why did God offer Job the opportunity to essentially "play God" in His answer to Job's complaint? How would this reveal the truth about God's unequalled greatness? How would it ultimately answer Job's complaint?

More to Consider: Most students agree that the animal described in Job 40:15–24 is the hippopotamus, although some prefer the elephant or the water buffalo. The word behemoth *is the transliteration of a Hebrew word that means "super-beast." Why did God choose such a beast in his answer to Job? How might that have intimidated Job? In today's society, a challenge about a hippo might not seem so difficult. How might God make the same point today if He were speaking to a modern-day Job?*

From the Commentary

Job knew he was beaten. There was no way he could argue his case with God. Quoting God's very words (Job 42:3–4), Job humbled himself before the Lord and acknowledged His power and justice in executing His plans (v. 2). Then Job admitted that his words had been wrong and that he had spoken about things he didn't understand (v. 3). Job withdrew his accusations that God was unjust and not treating him fairly. He realized that whatever God does is right, and man must accept it by faith.

Job told God, "I can't answer Your questions! All I can do is confess my pride, humble myself, and repent." Until now, Job's knowledge of God had been indirect and impersonal; but that was changed. Job had met God personally and seen himself to be but "dust and ashes" (v. 6; 2:8, 12; Gen. 18:27).

—*Be Patient*, page 188

10. What did Job's confession reveal about his heart? How did it reshape his frustration with his circumstances? With God? How might Job have then responded to his well-meaning but misguided friends?

Looking Inward

Take a moment to reflect on all that you've explored thus far in this study of Job 38—42. Review your notes and answers and think about how each of these things matters in your life today.

> *Tips for Small Groups: To get the most out of this section, form pairs or trios and have group members take turns answering these questions. Be honest and as open as you can in this discussion, but most of all, be encouraging and supportive of others. Be sensitive to those who are going through particularly difficult times and don't press for people to speak if they're uncomfortable doing so.*

11. Have you experienced a revelation of God? How did that compare to knowledge about God? How do you share the truth of God's revelation with someone who hasn't experienced something similar?

12. God essentially told Job, "You're not Me." Have you ever felt like you knew better than God in some area of life? What prompted that arrogance? How did that situation turn out? What role does God's mystery play in your understanding of Him and His purposes?

13. Think about a time when God humbled you. What led to that humbling? Why do you think God chose to humble you in this way? What did you learn from it about yourself? About God?

Going Forward

14. Think of one or two things that you have learned that you'd like to work on in the coming week. Remember that this is all about quality, not quantity. It's better to work on one specific area of life and do it well than to work on many and do poorly (or to be so overwhelmed that you simply don't try).

Do you need to be humbled before God? Be specific. Go back through Job 38—42 and put a star next to the phrase or verse that is most encouraging to you. Consider memorizing this verse.

Real-Life Application Ideas: Job thought he knew a lot about God and His ways, but it turned out he missed a few things. While our knowledge of God will always be incomplete, it's still important for us to know as much about God as we can so we can better hear His voice and follow the paths He prepares for us. Use this week to study God's character by reading biblical accounts of His intervention in the world. Don't forget the most important intervention of all—Jesus' birth, life, crucifixion, and resurrection. Then spend time in prayer, asking God to reveal the truth about Him that goes beyond knowledge.

Seeking Help

15. Write a prayer below (or simply pray one in silence), inviting God to work on your mind and heart in those areas you've noted above. Be honest about your desires and fears.

Notes for Small Groups:

- *Look for ways to put into practice the things you wrote in the Going Forward section. Talk with other group members about your ideas and commit to being accountable to one another.*
- *During the coming week, ask the Holy Spirit to continue to reveal truth to you from what you've read and studied.*

Summary and Review

Notes for Small Groups: This session is a summary and review of this book. Because of that, it is shorter than the previous lessons. If you are using this in a small-group setting, consider combining this lesson with a time of fellowship or a shared meal.

Before you begin ...
- *Pray for the Holy Spirit to reveal truth and wisdom as you go through this lesson.*
- *Briefly review the notes you made in the previous sessions. You will refer back to previous sections throughout this bonus lesson.*

Looking Back

1. Over the past eight lessons, you've examined the book of Job. What expectations did you bring to this study? In what ways were those expectations met?

2. What is the most significant personal discovery you've made from this study?

3. What surprised you most about Job's complaints and his friends' answers? What, if anything, troubled you?

Progress Report

4. Take a few moments to review the Going Forward sections of the previous lessons. How would you rate your progress for each of the things you chose to work on? What adjustments, if any, do you need to make to continue on the path toward spiritual maturity?

5. In what ways have you grown closer to Christ during this study? Take a moment to celebrate those things. Then think of areas where you feel you still need to grow and note those here. Make plans to revisit this study in a few weeks to review your growing faith.

Things to Pray About

6. Job is more than a book about suffering, but this theme is one that hits close to home with many people. As you reflect on the lessons you learned from reading Job, consider how they can help you to trust God even in times of great trials.

7. The messages in Job include learning patience, acknowledging God's greatness, and learning to trust in a God who is ultimately unknowable. Spend time praying for each of these topics.

8. Whether you've been studying this in a small group or on your own, there are many other Christians working through the very same issues you discovered when examining the book of Job. Take time to pray for each of them, that God would reveal truth, that the Holy Spirit would guide you, and that each person might grow in spiritual maturity according to God's will.

A Blessing of Encouragement

Studying the Bible is one of the best ways to learn how to be more like Christ. Thanks for taking this step. In closing, let this blessing precede you and follow you into the next week while you continue to marinate in God's Word:

May God light your path to greater understanding as you review the truths found in the book of Job and consider how they can help you grow closer to Christ.